D0318323

Cover illustration and Builders' Graveyard cartoon: Siôn Jones

ISBN: 0 86243 772 5

y **L***olfa*

Printed and published in Wales by
Y Lolfa Cyf., Talybont, Ceredigion SY24 5AP
e-mail ylolfa@ylolfa.com
website www.ylolfa.com
tel (01970) 832 304
fax 832 782

FOREWORD

South Wales was the first Klondyke in the world. At the turn of the 18th century, the industrial revolution was beginning to spread its flames from the first embers on to the roaring fires that fed the new iron age and gave a hint of the kingdom of coal to come.

Attracted to this new dawn came thousands of people. Hamlets became villages, villages became towns, and towns became an urban sprawl. It was a melting pot of humanity. This massive mix of humanity gradually but inexorably moulded itself into a new tribe (admittedly, it was a kind of mongrel society, but I've always had a lot ot time for mongrels – generally they're loyal and fairly clean around the house). Where once the Silures tribe had upped and given a good account of themselves in fixtures against the Romans, there now flourished a new multi-ethnic grouping – Valley Man... and Woman.

Valley Man has, over two centuries, stamped his mark on the ridges and thoughts that make up the terrain. As a group they became formidable, individually they attainted a certain personality trait. Any man fortunate enough to have this quality to an established and recognised degree, was accepted within his community, and without – as a character.

Now, many would say that the modern 21st century in its philosophy and stance, does not allow for characters – but if you venture forth, north of Cardiff, Newport and Swansea, you will, on a clear night, when the wind is right, still come upon them in their domain – the Valleys. David Jandrell is a kind of scout who still finds these characters regularly in their own habitat. From his own campus at Cwmcarn he has sallied forth and, with success, tapped in to the immediate warmth, abundant common sense, easy enquiring mind and exuberant humour of the unleashed, unfettered Valley Man.

In this book, David Jandrell's tales abound with the simplistic but effective wisdom of the Cwmcarn elders and his ear has been a Jodrell Bank of a receptor to record and relate the profound statements and philosophical arrows that fill the air in this region of Wales.

John Edwards of Abercynon, and of *Talk Tidy* fame was the first to pinpoint Wenglish as an established tongue. He has got the word into many dictionaries and I'm sure he'll get it recognised by the United Nations and the European Union eventually, so full credit goes to him. In his section of this unique region – the valleys of South Wales, David Jandrell proves that he, too, knows his people and has set out to record their sayings and doings.

For all of you who have a gap in your education and have so far failed to appreciate Valley Man, this book will cement that gap. For all who know Valley Man well – and may even be one – enjoy revelling again in a wee bit of self-indulgence, self-praise and yes, even self-criticism. It's good to talk, it's good to listen and in doing both, read on in David's book, so that you have some recall, perhaps, of what you said, how you said it and, if you didn't say it, surely you must know someone who did. Let David be your scout.

Roy Noble, 2005

Welsh Valley Characters: where to find them and how to spot them

"Let's go to Wales shall we?" I hear you say. You've heard so much about it, seen things on the telly; met Welsh people on holiday, nice enough. "Yeah, let's go there for a day out, or maybe even for our main holiday."

Wales: the land of song, mountains, lakes, scenery, beaches and… many surprises.

From whichever direction you enter the country, you will see breathtaking examples of all of the things you've heard about and were expecting to see: mountains, lakes, scenery, beaches and… funny road-signs: words that are three yards long, without a vowel to be seen! Still, there's a translation in English as well, so you'll be alright.

"Mummy, mummy, is there a spelling mistake on that sign?"
"Don't be silly, dear, road signs don't have spelling mistakes; it's probably written in Welsh."

So, you've done all the sights, been to all the 'touristy' places – the Beacons, the coast, Snowdonia, lakes, waterfalls, Cardiff. You've seen the Millennium Stadium, you've eaten chips in Caroline Street, and you've had a pint of SA, what next?

A trip to the valleys is not normally on the agenda for visitors to Wales, but such a venture can prove to be a delight for those who hail from 'over the bridge'. What will you see? Mountains, lakes, scenery? Yes, but not as 'in your face' as the ones that you see in the brochures. Hidden behind the long terraces, huge buildings, and churches that were once occupied by generations of miners, are the rolling hills and ice-cut valleys, lakes, waterfalls and scenery, beautiful enough to bring tears to your eyes.

Stop off and have a look. Valley villages are set in idyllic surroundings, apparently only known to the locals, who spend their spare time walking their dogs on picture-postcard-quality mountains, fishing in crystal clear streams, all only a stone's throw from their front doors.

Since the demise of the mining industry, all the old workings, and evidence of industrialisation have now disappeared, and the areas they occupied have been reclaimed, landscaped and brought back to their original natural beauty.

Wildlife can be seen all around, birds of prey circle way above our heads, even red kites have started to re-colonise some areas; herons stalk the rivers and streams, and some say that red squirrels have been seen scurrying up and down trees, hoarding nuts ready for the winter; characters, foxes and badgers hunt for smaller mammals and…

What are these characters, then?

Characters inhabit Welsh valley villages. They will be everywhere you look, and everywhere you turn. You can't get away from them, and, in most cases, you probably wouldn't want to get away from them. Characters actually define what the villages and communities are all about; it will be difficult to imagine such places without any.

After studying villages, in the search for characters, it suddenly became more interesting to investigate 'groups' of characters, rather than to isolate and single out people who are a bit eccentric and regarded by many as being 'oddballs'. All villages have at least one of those.

The study has revealed that the characters that exist in one village will actually exist in the next village, and the next, and the next, and so on.

So, who are these 'groups' of characters? Certainly, the inhabitants of a community will not notice anything untoward about any of the people with whom they share the village; neither will they notice anything strange if they go to a neighbouring village. These groups 'blend in' and their traits go unnoticed. It's as if the things that go on are natural to locals. They are accepted, and life goes on without so much as a raised eyebrow.

For the visitor, however, the behaviour of the characters in these groups can appear very odd indeed. Some may even be shocked when they first come into contact with characters. It is very important, therefore, for them to understand where these characters are 'coming from' and to have an insight into the kinds of things that can happen, so that they know how to deal with situations as they arise.

We will investigate the natural habitats of these characters and identify the best places to go to see them in action. We will look at the typical behaviour of characters, and realise that, in most cases, all 'goings on' will be in good faith and no offence intended. We will enter the places in which they operate, and experience first-hand the types of things that you can expect to see and hear when you join them in their own environment.

I cannot guarantee that visitors will encounter *all* the characters who have been investigated, nor will they experience any as extreme as those that are mentioned here, but, well, let's have a look, shall we?

Drinking and Watering Holes

Drinking is a very popular pastime in the South Wales Valleys. Quite a lot of this goes on in people's homes, but for those who choose to go out, there are generally two establishments that are frequented – the pub and the club. Most villages will have at least one of each of these, some will have more!

Pubs and Clubs

The clubs come under very different guises; they can be political – the Labour Club, the Conservative Club. They may be community based – the Workmen's Club, the Social Club; they may have a military connection – The British Legion Club, the Ex-Serviceman's Club; and sports-based – the Rugby Club, the Snooker Club.

So, whatever your political views may be, or your choice of sport, or your chosen career, there will be a 'watering hole' that you can visit that will be frequented by like-minded people. Strangely enough, if a village has only one club, a Labour Club for instance, it will be frequented by Labour supporters, Tories, Plaid members, Liberals, rugby boys, soccer boys, ex-servicemen, current servicemen, never-have-been-nor-never-will-be servicemen, and Uncle Tom Cobley and all.

Why is it, then, with so many establishments available to cater for just about every person's politics, sport, or vocation, that they congregate in the same one? Is it because it is too far to travel to get to your particular club? No, the reason is far simpler than that – the beer is cheaper in clubs than it is in pubs. Yes, cheap beer breaks down all barriers between rival factions. This is why staunch Socialists and Tories, Cardiff City and Swansea City fans, ex WWII soldiers and Italian Café owners can stand shoulder to shoulder at the bar and chat all night with never a mention of their differences.

Committees

Clubs are usually run by committees. The number of committee members per club is not fixed, but may be governed by the number of badges that the club has when selecting a new committee. Most badges simply display the word "Committee", but senior members' badges will be more ornate and will identify the Treasurer, Secretary, Chairman etc. This is different from pubs, of course. Pubs are run by the landlord/landlady and his/her name will appear above the front door. They organise all the events, decide who comes in and who doesn't, everything, in fact, that goes on within their walls. In short, they're the boss. In clubs, there are several bosses: The Committee.

In pubs, the landlord and landlady (the bosses) are usually behind the bar, and may sometimes be unaware of minor infringements of house rules, or boisterous behaviour that may be going on in the bar, if they are concentrating on serving in the lounge. Consequently, people who misbehave in any way in a pub have a fair chance of getting away with it. In clubs, getting away with even the slightest misdemeanour is virtually impossible. This is because the bosses are scattered throughout

GAMBLING, SPITTING and SWEARING, STRICTLY FORBIDDEN.

the building and are ready to pounce, unceremoniously, on any person who dares to break club rules.

You can be pulled up for crimes as heinous as swearing, cheating at cards, talking during bingo, standing by the bar after you've been served, and sitting in someone's seat. Sitting in someone's seat? Never underestimate the power of 'someone's seat'. A stranger in a club may experience dirty looks, or even abuse, if he goes to sit in what appears to be a vacant seat. In reality, the seat will be vacant, but the stranger will be unaware that the seat he has chosen is one that is normally frequented by a regular, and is, therefore, 'out of bounds'.

A stranger may have occupied 'someone's seat' and it may have gone unnoticed by the rest of the club members. In this case, the first time that the stranger becomes aware of the misdemeanour will be when he looks up and finds someone standing in front of him, pint in hand, with a very stern look on his face. This is the 'you're in my seat' stance. This stance can also incorporate the free (non-pint) hand on a hip, and a rapid tapping of the opposite foot. This usually prompts the stranger into initiating conversation, usually to try to ascertain why such aggressive eye contact is being made. This is a typical conversation that is heard under such circumstances:

"What's wrong with you?"

"You'm sat in my seat!"

"But I've been sat here all night!"

"You'm sat in my seat!"

Conversations of this nature rarely go on longer than this. Even though it may be ten minutes before 'stop tap', and the stranger has been in the club since 'open tap', and there may be several other vacant seats available, the stranger will eventually have to concede and go to sit somewhere else.

One incident tells of a stranger who went into a very busy club, bought a pint and went to sit in the only vacant seat in the bar. When it became apparent that the stranger was about to assume the 'sitting position' by the seat, screams of horror shook the building! He was told in no uncertain terms that he was about to sit in Bert's seat. The stranger seemed unperturbed by this barrage of abuse and announced that he'd get up and move when Bert came in. A man with a committee badge on had a quiet word with him and explained:

"Bert won't be coming in, he's dead. But when he was alive, he always sat in that seat. Nobody has sat in that seat for fourteen years, and that's the way it's gonna stay. It's a shrine to Bert, that seat is."

So, there are many things that you need to be aware of

when going into clubs, the matter of seats being just one. It is a good idea to make sure that you are aware of all rules and regulations and be sure that, if you conduct yourself in a manner that is likely even to approach infringing any of them, you will be pounced upon by any number of 'bosses' and dealt with accordingly – a letter from the committee.

Having your Beer Stopped

Letters from the committee can carry a number of penalties – the most severe being, 'having your beer stopped'. This is a rather confusing term that needs to be explained right away. If you've had 'your beer stopped', it means you've been banned from the establishment.

I had the term explained to me when I was about seventeen. I had been given the 'your beer is stopped' notice, and didn't regard it as a big problem as I was on cider in those days. A group of committee men explained the term in more detail, when I popped in for a few pints on the day after being sentenced. It's a good job that the authorities weren't aware that a seventeen-year-old had managed to con his way into membership of the club, or they would have had their beer stopped, as well!

In pubs, a different version of 'having your beer stopped' is used. A commonly used phrase, which means the same thing, is, "You're banned, mate, and don't come back in here again, not so long as my name is over the door, anyhow."

Banned

There is usually a group of people who find that their behaviour and reputations have led to them being banned from all the pubs in the locality. It is very interesting to note that

"Let's drink up and go somewhere else. The language in here is absolutely disgusting!"

they will all be spotted, out drinking and enjoying themselves together, at a particular event. This event is not common but does occur from time to time. There may even be years in between occurrences, but you can be sure that all banned folk will attend it.

The event in question is the first time that a new landlord takes over a pub from which they have been banned, and opens his doors to meet his new clientele. Regulars at these establishments are generally not overjoyed to see this influx of people who have been banned from their local, and are very quick to 'tell tales' on them to the new landlord.

"Oi, you don't wanna let 'im in here; blinkin' nuisance, he is. Banned from everywhere, mun! Oh aye, nothin' but trouble."

Sometimes, the landlord doesn't have to wait long to see evidence of these accusations for himself. Quite often, these people have been banned from establishments for fighting, usually with each other. In these cases, they may suddenly realise that this is the first time they've seen their adversaries since the fracas that got them banned in the first place. It is not unknown, in these circumstances, for a continuation of the original scrap to break out, when quite a lot of ale has been consumed, resulting in another ban, lasting until the next landlord takes over.

Here we see another common event. This normally occurs immediately after the 'scrappers' have been ejected. It involves the 'snitchers', who only moments before warned the landlord of imminent trouble, placing one elbow on the bar, leaning forward towards the landlord, with one eyebrow raised. This is the "See, I told you, didn't I?" stance, and, surprisingly, it precedes the words, "See, I told you, didn't I?"

Apart from these rather rare occurrences, things are pretty quiet in village pubs and clubs. Weeks come and go and the activities carry on as normal. Pool, darts, and cards leagues generally operate throughout the week nights, leaving Friday, Saturday and Sunday nights free for 'bigger' events, such as karaoke, discos and live bands.

Whichever establishment you choose to use, be it the pub or the club, whether you drink during the week, or just on the weekend, one thing is certain: you will be in an environment where you will come into contact with 'characters'.

Yes, pubs and clubs are generally the richest source of characters in the valley, and it is worth looking at the types of characters that are most commonly found.

The Landlord

Probably the 'biggest' and most prominent character in the local will be the landlord himself. The landlord has to wear several hats during the hours of opening. He may be required to compile and ask questions for the pub quiz, act as marriage guidance counsellor, free balls that are stuck in the pool table, be an expert on legal and medical matters, make sandwiches for the darts and cards teams, and for wedding receptions, settle arguments, be an expert on anything other than legal and medical matters, laugh at every joke told over the bar, whether he's heard them before or not, be a shoulder to cry on, be an expert on everything else and serve drinks.

The landlord will be the most clued-up on gossip of anyone in the village. He will know who's seeing whom, who shouldn't be seeing whom, but is anyway, who isn't seeing whom but is claiming to be seeing them, who has been seeing whom and wished they had never bothered, and be informed of all the sordid details of what went on during these 'sordid' liaisons. He will also be aware of all the stuff that's been pinched around the village, and will almost certainly know who pinched it. The chances are that he's been offered these goods over the bar, at real 'knock down' prices. He may even have purchased some of these goods, in good faith, of course.

Try to picture the look on a landlord's face when:

- he is trying to conceal a stolen item that he has just bought, by attempting to manoeuvre it under the bar, from his side, with his foot, so that the true owner,

- he doesn't catch a glimpse of it, while, at the same time, ranting to him about the theft of the item, and running through what he will do to the person who pinched it, when he catches him, whilst,

- the thief, who is drinking in rounds with the owner, is making desperate eye-contact with the landlord, warning him to 'keep shtoom' about it, before trying to 'change the subject by suggesting they both go and have a game of pool.

I wonder how many times that has happened?

This highlights one of the greatest skills in landlording: knowing when to say nothing.

Ladders

By far, the most common 'bargain' items that I have been offered in pubs, over the years, are ladders. There has never been a shortage of ladders on the valley black-market; apart from the shortage experienced by those who have had theirs pinched. That was, of course, during the 'Great Ladder Glut of 1978'. I have never been much of a ladder-man myself; I don't like heights, I don't even like being this tall (and I'm only five foot eight), so I was not moved to show any interest in a particular ladder that I was offered one night. The ladder in question was one of these extendable ones that come in three pieces. The 'seller' informed me that, although it was originally in three pieces, it had now been split. Two of the halves had already 'gone', and I was being given first refusal on the '*third half*'. I declined the offer, on the grounds that even the third half of a ladder was far too high for my liking, and I was immediately offered an alternative: a step-ladder, which was also on the market. I managed to decline that offer as well, by stating that I already had a step-ladder, as a result of our *real* ladder leaving home when we were kids.

Pub Experts

An example of why a landlord should be an expert on law is illustrated by the following story.

A stranger went into a pub and the landlord greeted him with the phrase,

"What are you having?"

The stranger asked for a beer and began slurping it down as soon as the landlord placed it on the bar. The landlord asked for £2.10, which was the price of a pint. The stranger informed the landlord that he wouldn't be paying for it as he had interpreted the term, "What are you having?" as an offer to 'have one on the house'. The landlord ensured him that the term was *not* an invitation to have a free pint, but the stranger disagreed with him, saying that anyone who wanted to buy someone a pint in a pub would use the phrase, "What are you having?"

At the other end of the bar, another man, who had been listening to the argument, piped up with, "He's right, you know. He could quite easily have misunderstood that phrase and assumed that you were going to buy him a pint. If you took him to court over it, you'd probably lose."

By this time, the landlord was fed up with the whole thing and told the stranger to drink up and leave.

The next day, the landlord could not believe it when he looked up and saw the stranger standing by the bar, waiting to be served. They had a little conversation. It went like this,

"Well, you can get out, for a start!"

"That's no way to greet a new customer."

"New customer! You were in here yesterday!"

"I wasn't."

"You were. You scrounged a free pint out of me!"

"I've never been in this pub before in my life."

"You were in here yesterday!"

"Excuse me, I am a travelling salesman and I am lost. I have only come in here to ask for directions. Not only have I never been in this pub before, I've never even been in this area before."

"Well if you've never been in this pub before, you must have a double!"

"Oh, that's very decent of you. I'll have a whisky, then, please."

Now, if the landlord had been 'up' on the law, he wouldn't have been swayed by the man who sided with the stranger and suggested that, if it went to court, the landlord would lose. Landlords must always be one step ahead of 'pub experts', because these can be the most dangerous characters you can encounter.

Pubs are full of potential experts, all ready to crawl out of the woodwork and bombard you with their advice on topics that they, usually, know nothing about. The cue for them to spring into action is the moment of realisation that you are seeking advice on something that you don't know anything about.

Punters put their lives on the line when they go into pubs and relate a problem that they may be having, or have come into contact with something they don't understand. Before they know it, there will be a queue of people ready to give advice and explain exactly what they will have to do to overcome their problems.

The following list shows the most popular topics covered by pub experts.

- Medical matters
- Motor mechanics
- DIY
- Anything else, if they are confident that you don't know enough about it to challenge them when they are talking a load of old codswallop

The people who are most at risk from 'pub advice', are those who are suffering from ill-health and are daft enough to 'make it known' to fellow drinkers. Any mention that you are a bit 'under the weather' will be regarded as an open invitation to a grilling on your symptoms and 'when you first noticed it'. Sufferers who are willing to share information on their symptoms will be treated to a barrage of sharp intakes of breath, shaking of heads and furrowed brows. Shortly after describing symptoms, the sufferer will start to receive diagnoses from the rest of the customers. These will cover the whole range of medical science known to, well, those in the pub, anyway. Someone complaining of a pain in his finger will be offered diagnoses from a list of conditions, ranging from a splinter, chilblains, double diphtheria, hepatitis 'K' to plague.

In fact, not one medical condition that has been mentioned on *Casualty*, *Peak Practice*, or the *Open University*, over the last ten years, will be left out of the list of possible diseases of which the pain in the finger may be a symptom. When you bear in mind the number of programmes that the *Open University* broadcasts these days, there are plenty of other subjects that can also provide 'conditions' that have been used in diagnoses. Take Art for example. A person going into a pub, fresh from watching an Art programme, may well diagnose Cubism as a possible reason for someone who is feeling a bit 'under the weather', or may simply put it down to the sufferer 'going through a bit of a Blue Period'.

Whatever the final diagnosis is, the prognosis will certainly be grim. A very bleak future faces a person who has been 'examined' in the bar, and the sufferer will be faced with the thought that he has no more than a fortnight left to live, and the end will be slow, painful and very, very messy. I heard of one person who was given a fortnight by the punters in the bar. Not happy with this, he went into the dart room for a second opinion, to see if he could get a month out of them. Another chap, given a fortnight, asked if he could have the last week of July and the first week of August. He loved the Miners' Fortnight in Trecco. Oh aye, loved it, he did!

People who are equally at risk from the experts are those who are suffering an affliction but have been to see the doctor *before* consulting the people in the bar. These will be quizzed as to the nature of the treatment they are receiving, and the responses will be met with a barrage of sharp intakes of breath, shaking of heads and furrowed brows. Of course, according to the 'experts', the treatment given will be totally inappropriate, and no one will be backward in coming forward with an alternative.

Whatever the illness or affliction, the 'new' remedies can all be 'knocked up' in an average kitchen. The remedies will consist mainly of bicarb. The other ingredients will vary according to the nature and severity of the disease. Vinegar is also a very popular 'cure-all' ingredient: "Oh aye, our mam drank a pint of vinegar and bicarb every day till she died. Never done her any harm!"

The main risk for these sufferers is if they decide to take the advice of their drinking mates and ignore the treatments prescribed by their doctors. Sufferers who do switch to the alternative, may find that they become much more susceptible to a life expectancy of a fortnight than those mentioned previously.

Doctor: "I don't think we've been taking our tablets, have we, Mr. Jenkins?"

Mr. Jenkins: "No doctor, I've been dancing around naked in the wood at midnight when there's a full moon, and shoving raw liver into a knothole in an oak tree, after tying nettles around my head. Oh, and I've been drinking pints of bicarb and vinegar. Mrs. Thomas swore by it. Did that every day, right up until the time she died."

Of hypothermia and bicarb and vinegar poisoning, no doubt!

I can think of only one instance of a person who might have benefited more from seeking advice from the pub advisors, rather than choosing the method he did. The unfortunate gent was suffering with piles, and had gone to the doctor for help. The doctor gave him a prescription for suppositories and told him to follow the instructions on the box. When he got home, he checked the instructions, which read,

'Place two suppositories up the rectum each day.'

Unfortunately, he was not familiar with the term 'rectum', so he looked it up in a dictionary. The dictionary definition for 'rectum' was: 'the back passage', so, every day, he took two suppositories out of the box, took them down the back passage and left them on the table behind the back door.

After three months, he looked at the mound of mouldy suppositories on the table and decided that they were doing his condition no good at all. He went back to see his doctor.

"Doctor, those blinkin' tablets you gave me was useless. I've used 'em all up, and my piles is blinkin' worse. I may as well have stuck 'em up my arse!"

Motor Mechanics

Another subject that is very popular with pub experts is motor mechanics. If you have a problem with your car, it is best not to mention it in passing, when waiting to be served, otherwise the experts will pounce. They will generally be the same experts that give their medical advice, and they have already been dealt with. So, if your car is 'knocking' when you are driving along, a number of things could be causing the irritating noise. First of all, an expert will give his opinion on what the cause is, and this will be shot down, immediately, by the other experts, who wish to give their advice.

Knocking whilst driving, according to experts, can be put down to the carburettor, petrol pump, starter motor, fan belt, oil sump, prop shaft, steering column, clutch, brake fluid, windscreen washers, radiator, wing mirrors, petrol cap, sun roof, fuel injection – in fact, the list will only be limited by the number of people in the pub who are 'thinking them up'.

The more astute expert will conclude that your problem is probably a combination of some of the above; maybe even a combination of all of the above, with a few others as well, just to be on the safe side. If you decide not to take the advice of the experts, and say you're going to take it to a garage, just in case it's 'something else', the next inquest will begin.

- "Where are you taking it, then?"
- "Oooh, you don't want to take it to them, mun; cowboys, they are!"
- "I wouldn't trust them to blow up the tyre on my wheelbarrow!"
- "Blinkin' crap, they are, and expensive."
- "I wouldn't bother with them, don't know nothing about cars, they don't, I'll tell you the best place to go to. You know the garage by the lights, well, not them; the others, down the road a bit."

It will not be long before you realise that there is not an establishment capable of replacing even a wiper blade within a 20-miles radius of your home, as every garage recommended by one expert will immediately be pooh-poohed by another. There will also be a plethora of half-offers to repair the vehicle from fellow drinkers.

- "Of course, I'd love to have a look at it for you, trouble is, I'm up to my nuts in it at the moment."
- "The only time I can have a look at it is Saturday morning, but I can't, because I've got to take the missus to ASDA, otherwise I would."
- "I'll have a look at it Sunday. What time can you pick me up? Oh, you can't, can you, 'cos your car's knackered. Better leave it then."
- "I'll do it; not a problem. Now, let's see… er… three weeks Thursday, okay?"

Sometimes, these advisors are so confident about their knowledge that they operate outside the walls of the pub. One chap, Bob, had given so much advice on car mechanics that he believed that he could actually do the job. He managed to bluff his way through an interview, and got a job as a car mechanic at a local garage. On his first morning, the boss asked Bob to change the gearbox on a vehicle that was parked on the forecourt. He drove the car into the workshop, lifted the bonnet and stared blankly at all the 'workings' underneath. It just looked like scrap metal and spaghetti to him. He placed his thumb on the biggest lump of metal he could see, and hit it as hard as he could with a mallet. Bob ran into the office with his newly flattened thumb and told the boss he'd had an accident and would have to go on the sick. The boss couldn't believe how unlucky his new employee

"Hello, I've got a Beetle here, and I'm wondering if you can take a look at it for me!"

was for having such a bad accident on his first day, and told him to take as much time off as he needed to get his thumb 'up and running' again.

After three months, our chap reported in to the boss, 'fit for duty' again. The boss was pleased to see him back as they were very busy, and told Bob to change the gearbox on a vehicle that was parked on the forecourt. Bob was still clueless on what to do, and as the forecourt was on a slight gradient, he slipped the handbrake off and let the vehicle roll over his foot.

Bob limped into the office with his newly flattened foot and told the boss he'd had another accident and that he'd have to go on the sick again! The boss was absolutely flabbergasted and told Bob he was probably the unluckiest person he'd ever met. He told Bob to take as much time off as he needed to get fit again.

Three months later, Bob reported in 'fit for duty'. The boss was very pleased to see him and asked Bob to change the gearbox on a vehicle that was parked on the forecourt. Bob couldn't stand it any longer. He looked the boss straight in the eye and asked,

"Am I the only mechanic working here that knows how to change gearboxes?"

I felt sorry for Bob when I heard about that.
I didn't have any sympathy at all, however, for the 'proper' mechanic who spent all one morning exchanging a perfectly good gearbox for a new one, forgetting he was working on his own car!

DIY

DIY is also a topic covered widely in pubs. People often go into pubs to relax and unwind after a hard slog on a DIY problem, and are always keen to share their difficulties with other people who are drinking there at the time. The main danger area here arises if the storyteller has not yet solved the problem. Now is the time for the experts to change into DIY mode and bombard the unfortunate 'DIYer' with:

- "…aaaah, you see, that's where you went wrong."
- "Oh, no, you don't want to do it like that, mun."
- "You'll never do it if you try to do it that way. Now, what you want to do is…"
- "Yes, I'm a big fan of Do It Yourself. If anyone asks me to do something, I always say 'Do It Yourself'."

The 'DIYer' cannot really win in this situation. If he's stuck on a certain project, there will be 101 different theories on offer on how to sort it out. The people who have offered these theories will argue their points vehemently amongst themselves and use the poor 'DIYer' as the arbitrator. If the 'DIYer' has completed the job, there will always have been a better way. It could have been done in half the time and much cheaper:

"Why didn't you say, mun. I've got one of them, if you had said, you could have had it."

Unless the 'DIYer' is a craftsman, or is very 'handy', he may well find it expedient to cut all this out and seek help from a *real* expert in the field, who may present more problems than all 'pub experts' put together. This is an entirely unique beast and is a law unto himself: the Builder.

The Builder

Builders tend to conduct most of their business in pubs. They can obtain jobs, recruit labour and source materials, all in the pub, and in the time it takes to play a game of pool.

Builders can be very popular people in a pub, during an evening session, as there is always someone who wants a wall built at the bottom of the garden, has a slate off the roof, wants some shelves put up, a leaky window, etc. They maintain their popularity by saying, "Well, I've got a big job on in Newport in the morning, but I'll drop the boys off and I'll come up personally and sort it out for you. Should be there at… ooooh… 11 o'clock at the latest. Don't worry. I won't charge you anything, just get me a pint in sometime. Oh, go on, then. Thanks very much."

During the course of one evening, it is not unreasonable for a builder to claim to be able to drop the boys off at the important job in Newport, and, no later than 11 o'clock, to be at:

Mrs. Jenkins', to fix a dripping tap
Mrs. Jones', to repair the shed
Mr. Thomas', to bleed a radiator
Mrs. Price's, to unblock the sink
Mrs. Evans', to replace the skirting
Mrs. Davies', to build a kennel
Mrs. Griffiths', to put up a dado rail
Mr. Morgan's, to shift some rubble
Mrs. Lewis', to put up a pelmet
Mrs. Williams', to move the Sky dish

Usually, the builder is at none of these locations by 11 o'clock the next day. In fact, it is unlikely that he will actually turn up at *one* of them. Excuses will range from:

- "The van broke down."
- "One of the lads didn't turn up and I had to stay on the job."
- "I came around and couldn't get an answer."
- "Something cropped up."
- "I had to take the dog to the vet."
- "I couldn't remember your address."
- "I cut my finger and had to go to the hospital."
- "We managed to get the van going and it broke down again."

In the very unlikely event that the builder does show up for one of the appointments, the format of the meeting will be along these lines: He will occupy the most comfortable armchair in the house, and go on and on about the pressures associated with the 'big job in Newport', the cost of materials, the men he has working for him, the fact there are not enough hours in the day, the van breaking down, the weather stopping them working outside, the skip not being delivered on time, and anything else that crops up during his stay. He will continually flick dried cement from under his fingernails onto the carpet, and drop unsubtle hints for a cup of tea: "Cor, my throat isn't half dry this morning, Mrs Jenkins. Must be the weather, or could be the cement. Very dusty, see."

The 'tea capacity' of the builder is best measured in gallons, and he will sup as long as the supply continues. When it looks as if the supply is about to 'dry up' and there is no sign that the kettle is going to go back on, he will bring the 'meeting' to a close, by standing suddenly, giving his thighs a good slap, releasing two small clouds of dried cement, which will deposit itself evenly over the armchair, and announcing,

"Right, I'd best get myself down B&Q's, to get the stuff to do this. I'll be back in half an hour. Get the kettle on ready, and we'll have this job done before you know it."

Needless to say, as soon as he drives away, the van will break down, or he'll have to take the dog to the vet, or he won't be able to remember the address of the house he's just left, or he will have managed to get the van going and it went and broke down again! Well, he just won't come back. Trying to get an agreed job done? This can be one of the most difficult tasks that you may face in your lifetime. Once the initial visit to 'measure up' has happened, which usually constitutes about 16 broken appointments, the estimate will arrive. Take no notice whatsoever of the estimate, it will bear very little resemblance to the final price. The final price will never *ever* be *less* than the estimate!

So, the estimate is done, you're happy with it, and you get a start date. Before you begin to move furniture and lift carpets ready for the 'big start day', remember, it is always advisable to add at least 6 months to the promised start date, to allow for:

- The van breaking down
- The bad weather making it impossible to work outside, even though your job is inside
- Having to take the dog to the vet – because of a very long illness
- Forgetting your address
- Buying a new van because he'd had a gutful of the other one breaking down, and, lo and behold, the new one broke down
- Something else

Sometimes, during this waiting period, another builder will seize the opportunity and tempt you with "Don't bother with him, mun; too unreliable. I'll start the job tomorrow and get it done in two days. No problem."

Many people take up these offers and get the job done fairly quickly, but the after-sales service in the building trade seems to be fairly standard:

- "No, that's not damp; it's condensation, 'cos you've got a 'cold spot' over by there."
- "The shelf I put up is perfectly level. It looks 'out' 'cos of one of them 'optical collisions' as a result of the rest of the room not being square."
- "That crack in the plaster, running along the whole length of the room, is a perfectly normal occurrence during the drying out process."

Whatever the excuse, it will always end with the phrase, "So that's not down to me."

Sooner or later, right out of the blue, the *original* builder will arrive, unannounced, ready to do the job. When he sees that the job has been done, he will immediately use the phrase, "Well, who the Hell did this? WHO? I thought as much. Well, well, well, well, well. And how much did he charge? HOW MUCH? Well, well, well, well, well. I gotta be honest; I could have done this job ten times better, twice as quick and for half the price. Well, well, well, well, well. Cor, my throat isn't half dry this morning, Mrs. Jenkins; must be the weather, or could be the cement; very dusty, see. Oh, go on then, milk, two

sugars, please, and you haven't got any of your bake-stones, have you? Lovely, they are. I was telling my missus about them. Heard the latest on the van? No? Ooooh, you wouldn't believe it, mun…'

The Computer Expert

Another *real* expert to avoid in pubs is the 'computer expert', or IT expert, as they would prefer to be known. IT stands for 'Irritating Twit', I believe, but I can't be certain. Most households these days have computers, and for those who are not computer literate they can present major problems.

The instruction manuals are so complicated that they may as well be written in French, for the good that they do for the frustrated reader. But, never fear, because the good old software manufacturers have built 'HELP' files into the programmes; you can click on and they'll solve all your problems. Ha, ha, ha! The jargon used in both the manuals and the help files is so complicated that, if you could understand it, you wouldn't have any need to read them.

So, you have read and not understood a word of the jargon provided by the computer suppliers on how to solve your problem. Your computer is still not working; you go to the pub for a pint, and spot your friendly neighbourhood IT expert, standing at the bar.

You explain the problem as best you can, you try to include all the little messages that flash up and disappear before you get chance to read them all, and then try to explain as much as you can understand about what the manuals and HELP files said you should do.

You wait expectantly, whilst he takes a sip of his pint, and get ready for the diagnosis. Usually, the IT expert will explain the problem in fine detail. He will not use *any* of the complicated terminology that was provided by the manuals and HELP files, but will merely substitute for it even more complicated jargon, and ask you questions that only someone with a degree in computing or microelectronics would be able to answer.

Another common suggestion is, "Turn it off and turn it back on again, See if that works."

One of my favourites is, "Sounds to me like, either the machine doesn't like the disk, or the disk doesn't like the machine."

In this case, I think that the term "doesn't like", is not to be interpreted in the literal sense; it is more likely to be an IT term, meaning "I haven't got a clue what the problem is but I am not going to stand here and admit it in front of all these people. Instead, I am going to fob you off with a term that is absolutely meaningless. Now, please go away and quit bothering me."

Scuzzy

Once, I had the misfortune of standing at the bar, with IT experts either side of me. They talked IT all night – in the best jargon they could muster. I was very intrigued throughout the evening by the word 'scuzzy', which was being used at least three times in every sentence that went straight over my head. I thought it was a fantastic word and so I looked it up. Apparently, it means 'unkempt', according to the dictionary. I couldn't see what this had to do with computers, so I made further enquiries and discovered that the word was actually 'SCSI', and it is an acronym for 'Small Computer Systems Interface'.

I'm sorry, but SCSI is *not* scuzzy. Nevertheless, I think it's such a good word that I use it all the time when speaking to IT experts, whether it's appropriate or not. Some of the ways I have used it are:

My Phrase	*What it Means*
Not enough scuzz in it	A computer that is old and needs upgrading
Scuzzied right up to the hilt	A top of the range PC, the opposite of above
Scuzzed out of all proportion	Overcomplicated manuals and HELP files
Scuzzy board (bored)	Describes someone listening to an IT expert

"When I said I wanted a PC for Christmas…"

The Canine Show Judge

Another case of an expert who gave some advice which didn't quite 'do the trick' is told here:

A postman, who was also a 'canine show judge' in his spare time, was walking up the path to a house to deliver some mail. When he arrived at the door, just as he was about to deliver the letters, the door opened and the woman of the house put some milk bottles on the doorstep. They greeted each other and started to chat about the weather. During the chat, the postman noticed a little dog running around in the house. He looked at the dog and thought he recognised it as a Schnauzer.

He asked the woman if the little dog was a Schnauzer, and she confirmed that it was. The postman told her that the particular colouring of the dog made it very rare indeed and, if the dog was a pedigree, and she had all his papers, the dog could make thousands if she entered him for big shows like Cruft's.

She confirmed that the dog was a real pedigree, and she had all the papers to prove it. The postman was very excited and suggested that she removed some of the whiskers from the dog's face, as it would make the dog absolutely 'unbeatable' in a competition. The woman was over the moon with this news and told the postman that she'd shave them off right away and enter him for the first competition she could find.

The postman then informed her that the whiskers needed to be removed chemically, rather than shaved, because shaving merely made them grow back quicker and thicker. He told her that she should buy the strongest hair remover that was available and apply it liberally over the dog's snout.

As soon as the postman left, the woman got dressed and dashed to the chemist's and asked for the strongest stuff on the market. The chemist went into the back room and came back with a bottle. He put it on the counter, and before she could pick it up, he issued this warning:

"Right, madam, this is the strongest hair remover that has ever been produced. It is vicious! Before you use it, I must give you some advice, which you must follow to the letter. If you use it on your legs, do not wear stocking, or tights, or any clingy trousers. You must let the air circulate around it, or you could suffer burns. If you use it under your arms, do not wear any tight tops or blouses. It's best to wear singlets, or vests, for at least three weeks, in order to let the air get at it."

The woman thought about this for a moment and replied, "Actually, it's for my Schnauzer."

To which the chemist replied, "In that case, don't ride a bike for a fortnight."

The Pub Quiz

Whilst we have looked at the pub experts and their vast knowledge of just about everything, from time to time, pubs provide an opportunity for them to really show off their talents. This takes the form of the pub quiz.

So, eyes down, best of order, this is a very serious business, you know. Grab all your mates and huddle together in the corner. Make sure nobody else can hear you, or look over your shoulder, to get the answers.

Have a look at some of the answers offered in quizzes; they're all genuine!

And here we go… Question one…

Q. Where and when did the Great Fire of London start?
A. It started in London when a pudding caught fire.

Q. What is the name of the infamous Australian outlaw who wore a tin head shield?
A. Mick Jagger.

Q. What name is given to young fish?
A. Fried.

Q. What name do we give to a savage elephant? A clue is: Five letters beginning with 'R'.
A. Rhino?

Q. Which Duke defeated Napoleon at the Battle of Waterloo? A clue is:
A boot was named after this person.
A. Duke Ellington.

Q. What everyday item was invented by Lazlo Biro?
A. Baby plant food.

Q. What is Einstein most famous for?
A. His relatives.

Q. What fatty-based substance is applied to the hair to improve its condition?
A. Restructuring semen.

Q. Daley Thompson found fame as...?
A. A newspaper with telephone numbers in it.

Q. What does the term 'ANON' mean when seen at the end of a piece of writing?
A. It's when people want to remain unanimous.

Q. Princess Diana has recently returned home from...?
A. A six-day world tour of India.

Q. Who was the President of the NUM in 1974 when the miner's strike brought down the Heath Government?
A. Nat King Coal.

Q. What ailment is caused from a severe deficiency of Vitamin C?

A. Scurbies. Old sailing ships had them.

Q. Cervantes' most famous novel was called?

A. Donkey Horsey.

Q. How is data transferred from one computer to another?

A. They do it with wobbly discs.

Q. Why can't you re-freeze food once it's been defrosted and heated?

A. Because you can warm it up but you can't cold it down.

Q. How did Joan of Arc meet her death?

A. She was decaffeinated when her scarf got caught in a car door.

Q. How did Charles Edward the Young Pretender escape his pursuers in 1745?

A. By hiding in the Royal Oak pub. You can still see it on the left hand side if you go from Newport to Cardiff on the bus.

Q. How did John Quincy Adams meet his grisly end?

A. John Adams, also known as grisly, was eaten by a bear who he later tamed.

Q. Guy Fawkes is famous for what?

A. He tried to blow up Buckingham Palace on Bonfire night.

Q. What name is given to small Oriental fishing boats?

A. Tampons.

Q. Who were the Aztecs?

A. People who decorated ancient ceilings.

Q. Anaemia, a blood disorder is caused by...?

A. A lack of iron deficiency.

Q. Why do scientists believe that there may be water on the moon?

A. Because of the Sea of Tranquillity they found up there.

Q. What is 'Dry Ice'?
A. Frozen water placed in front of a fire. Genesis use it.

Q. What is a tropism?
A. A temporary permanent bend in a plant's stem.

Q. Finish this famous quotation, "They think it's all over..."
A. "Because I used to love her, but it's all over now."

Q. How many thousandths are there in an inch?
A. Millions.

Q. What was the 'Diet of Worms'?
A. An eating disorder, now obsolete.

Q. A pre-decimal coin, worth twelve and a half pence was called the "Half...."?
A. Quid.

Q. It is said that, "Everyone can remember what they were doing when...."?
A. They were born.

Watch out for the 'Speling Round'!

Q. What is the city of York well known for?
A. Couldn't even beat Newport County.

Q. What do UFOlogists study?
A. Ufes?

Q. What is Advocaat?
A. A type of anteater.

Q. "Four and twenty blackbirds baked into a pie". How many is 'four and twenty'?
A. Forty four.

Q. Stradivarius was famous for manufacturing which musical   instruments?
A. Fenders.

Q. King Henry VIII was famous for?
A. Being King.

Q. Extinction means?
A. Making sure you put your cigarettes out.

Q. Where do peanuts grow?
A. Monkey Puzzle trees.

Q. Distances at sea are measured in?
A. Fluid ounces.

Q. What is a capon?
A. A thing you put on your guitar to tighten the strings up with.

Q. Where would you find the 'Islets of Langerhans'? (In the Pancreas)
A. Greece.

* * *

One pub quiz story involves a question master who would not budge from the answer that was written on his sheet.

The question posed was, "What does a hygrometer measure?"

The team who had to answer that question came up with, "It measures humidity."

The question master said that the answer was incorrect, and was going to pass it over to the other team. Before he had chance to do this, the team that had just had their answer rejected, asked him to clarify if he had said 'hygrometer' or 'hydrometer'. He confirmed that he had said 'hygrometer' and the team said that they couldn't come up with a different answer because hygrometers measure humidity.

He offered it to the other team and they didn't know it.

Both teams were now on the edge of their seats, waiting for the question master to reveal the answer.

"And the *correct* answer is… it measures the amount of moisture in the atmosphere."

Despite complaints from both teams, he would not award a point on the basis that "It's not the answer that's on the sheet, so you can't have it."

* * *

This little gem was overheard in a bar, when a punter was trying to guess what sort of dog had just been purchased by another punter. He was given very good clues by the owner of the dog, but didn't seem to be catching on very quickly. The dog was a Yorkshire terrier.

"The answer consists of two words, the first word is the name of a place, and the second is the name of a dog."

"Like golden Labrador?"

"Yes, but 'golden' isn't the name of a place is it."

"No, nor Labrador isn't."

"Actually, Labrador is the name of a place, but, forget that for the time being. The clue for the first word is, Geoffrey Boycott."

"Who's he?"

"A cricketer."

"Who does he play for?"

"The answer to that is the name of the place, so I'll give you another clue."

"Go on then."

"Emmerdale."

"I know; it's a sheepdog."

"No."

"But they have sheepdogs on Emmerdale Farm!"

"But sheep isn't the name of a place, is it? I'll give you another: a pudding you eat with beef."

"Steak and kidney."

"That isn't a dog, is it?

"No."

"Okay, which county is Leeds in?

"Dunno."

"Which county is Sheffield in?"

"Dunno."

"This is a very big clue. Which county is York in?"

"Dunno."

"You don't know which county York is in?"

"No."

"Okay, then, which county is Monmouth in?"

"Gwent."

"No, it's in Monmouthshire."

"Oh."

"Which county is Leicester in?

"Dunno."

"Well if Monmouth is in Monmouthshire, then Leicester must be in…

"Leicestershire?"

"And Derby is in?"

"Derbyshire?"

"Right, so which county is York in?"

"Yorkshire. Oh, I know, Yorkshire Terrier!"

Gossips

Gossiping is a very big part of valley life, for some, the biggest part. The group of characters who gossip habitually do not restrict their activities to pubs; they can operate anywhere in the village, and no-one is exempt from it.

Gossiping is best noticed in places where there are queues: the Post Office, the Spar, the newsagent's, the Doctor's surgery, or where people congregate *en masse*: the café, church, buses/ bus stops etc.

It is surprising the amount of information that can be picked up by simply frequenting these places and observing. Of course, you will not pick up all the information that is being gossiped about, but you can get a fair idea of what's been going on and who's been doing it. You have to try to work out the full story from the snippets that you hear. You may have to visit several sources, and hope that the gossip is on the same topic, to get a fuller picture. You may even get names and dates, depending on how vigilant you are when gathering your information.

There will most certainly be gaps in the information you get, so, you do what everyone else does in this situation: make up the rest, so that the story flows. Easy, isn't it?

Even if there is a modicum of truth in a story, by the time it has been passed on a few times, it will be blown out of all proportion, and the story becomes so absurd that even Hollywood film moguls wouldn't dream of making a picture out of it.

So, if a vehicle, parked outside the newsagents at 8am, has its wing mirror clipped by a passing vehicle, by 4pm, it will be reported that there had been a multiple pile-up, the road would have been closed by police, not to mention the fatalities!

Sometimes, it can be fun to feed known 'gossips' with false information, in the hope that they will bite and 'start spreading the news'. I saw the opportunity once and grabbed it with both hands. I was walking down the street with a friend and saw that we were approaching a first class gossiper. As soon as we got within earshot of the 'target', I broke into the sentence that I was saying at the time and carried on with, "…Oooh aye, and they found him dead this morning. Dreadful it was. You'd expect it in America, but not in a little village like this. Can't believe it. I was only talking to him Friday, as well. It's a good job we don't know what's round the corner, that's for sure…"

As soon as we'd passed the gossiper, I went back to my original sentence and carried on from the point where I had left it.

The result of that little 'red herring' was exactly what had been intended. Needless to say, the village was buzzing with the excitement that someone had been murdered. Everybody was trying to find out who it was and where it had taken place. It was reported that, ten minutes after my 'comment' in the street, our gossiper was seen knocking doors, and she had got through three streets by the time villagers lost sight of her. When the first reports started to 'get around', a murder had taken place and, whilst there was no name available, they had narrowed the location down to one of three houses.

Later news filtered through that the victim had actually been named, and a motive was now being formulated. The motive was organised about an hour later, and, of course, once the motive was sorted, the identity of the murderer was just a matter of time. This particular 'matter of time' was 'open tap', when the bar was full of eager punters, all awaiting 'more news'. It seemed all very strange. There appeared to be no Police presence in the village, and what made it worse, the 'victim' had been spotted, not ten minutes earlier, going into the chip shop!

When a few of them noticed me in the bar, I was asked to relate the whole story from scratch, seeing as the original story had come from me, according to the chief gossip. I told them I didn't know a thing about it, and enquired as to why they thought the original story had come from me. When told that I had been overheard telling the story to my friend in the street, I cleared the whole thing up with, "Oh, that. Actually I was telling him a joke about a murder, and someone must have just caught part of it and thought it was real!"

Strangely enough, even though the 'truth was out', there were still those who talked about that murder for weeks afterwards. It seems that even a murder that never happened is much more interesting to talk about than a genuine mistake. Well, not so much a mistake, more like a genuine 'on purpose'.

Not only will gossips want to know everything, they will actually know enough about you to influence others, either for or against you, depending on how they're feeling at the time. To illustrate this, it is well worth recalling the story of the day when Malcolm wanted to mow his lawn and decided to ask

Bob, a neighbour, if he could borrow his lawnmower.

So, Malcolm was on his way to see Bob, and half way there, he bumped into Roger.

"Hello, Malc, where you off to, butt?"

"Off to see Bob."

"What d'you want him for?"

"I'm going to ask him if I can borrow his lawnmower."

"You gotta be blinkin' jokin', mun. He won't lend you sod all. Tight as hell, he is."

"Is he?"

"Aye, you got no chance. Save yourself the bother and go back home."

"Well, I'm half way there now. I'll see what he says."

"See you."

"*We have reason to believe that the murder weapon was a sharp instrument.*"

Roger walked off with a chuckle. Malcolm continued, and soon he bumped into Mike.

"Hiya, Malc. Off anywhere nice?"

"No, only down Bob's."

"Owes you money, does he?"

"No, I'm going to ask him if I can borrow his lawnmower."

"You haven't gone mad, have you? Bob won't lend nothing to nobody."

"Is that right?"

"You got no chance, mate!"

"Well, I'm here now. I can only ask."

As Malcolm was walking up Bob's path, he was thinking about the conversations he'd had with Mike and Roger. He remembered that Bob was pretty tight. Bob never had money or sweets, when they were in school. He borrowed from everyone, and never paid anything back. He knocked on Bob's door, and carried on thinking.

"Yes, I must be mad. I've asked him to lend me stuff before, never so much as got a penny out of him. Borrowed plenty off me, though. Never seen any of it back, though!"

At this point, Bob answered the door and greeted Malcolm with, "Hello, Malc. There's nice to see you. Comin' in for a cuppa?"

To which Malcolm replied, "As far as I'm concerned, you can stick your lawnmower up your arse!"

So, everyone will know everything about you, more than you'll ever realise. You will be the topic of discussion the moment you leave a room or a shop.

"Oh aye, he can talk! And did you see who he was with on Saturday night? And her a married woman an' all. Disgustin' it is. Brazen hussy. Mind you, I blame him. Always been the same, he has; blinkin' brains is in his trousers…!"

I've seen people get nearly to the front of a long queue in a shop, abandon their place and go to join the end of the queue, in the hope that by the time they get to the front of the queue again, the people who have been standing by the door, discussing each and every customer as they leave the shop, will have gone to 'hold court' somewhere else.

Gossips on Sex

By far the most popular 'discussion point' amongst gossips is sex; sex amongst people other than themselves, of course. They like to keep their own activities close to their chests, but will take whatever steps are required to find out about other people's antics.

The amount of interest generated by 'relationships' can be quantified by looking at the amount of effort that goes into finding out all the 'nitty-gritties', scored on a scale from 1 to 10. On this scale, 10 represents the maximum effort.

Score	Nature of Relationship
1	Long term relationship between two single people of the opposite sex.
2	One night stand between two single people of the opposite sex.
3	One night stand between two people of the opposite sex, one of which is married to someone other than the person they had the one night stand with.
4	One night stand between two people of the

opposite sex, both married to other people.

5   Any relationship involving more than two people.
        Whether any of them are single or married is not
        important.

6   Any relationship involving people of the same sex.

7   Any relationship involving people with an age
        difference of more than thirty years.

8   Any relationship involving two people, one of
        which is 'well known' and is also known to be
        attached to 'someone else'. E.g., Churchwarden,
        local policeman, rent man, teacher.

9   Any relationship involving two 'well known'
        people, both attached to someone else. E.g., Vicar
        and woman who works in the chip shop, dentist
        and secretary of the embroidery club, district
        nurse and the local Rotary club.

10   Any relationship between people who are related
        to each other.

So, if you are planning to form any relationship at all, try to develop one that does not fall into any of the categories above. Admittedly, it will be difficult, but remember that it will only be a matter of time before the cat will be out of the bag and you will be the topic of gossip that will last until someone else gets 'caught out'.

Don't make the mistake of going 'elsewhere' to 'carry on'. You may not even be safe in villages further up or further down the valley. Check the fixture lists of all darts, pool, cards and skittles leagues, paying particular notice to your pub's 'away' games. You don't want to be in a pub, canoodling with someone that you shouldn't be canoodling with, safe in the knowledge that no one knows you there, and you look up and see your local Crib and Don team striding into the bar for a cards match.

In the Public Arena...

Here are some stories that have been told regarding some 'relationships' that have become public knowledge, sadly for those that were involved.

Tudor, an 87-year-old, very rich gent, and Tracey, his 19-year-old and very attractive wife, went to see a marriage guidance counsellor, to see if they could get some advice on their disastrous lovemaking sessions.

"She just lies there, mun!" Tudor complained to the startled counsellor

"And your next number out... three and seven, thirty seven. Oh, and have a guess who was with Ron in the Rose and Crown in Ponty last Friday night, who, by the way, told his missus he was going to the King's Head for a pigeon meeting."

"Although I love him to bits, I just don't fancy him, see," said Tracey.

After considering the matter for a while, the counsellor proposed a solution. He suggested that, as Tudor was not short of a few bob, he hire one of the lads from the local rugby team to 'assist' in their sessions. Tudor was to pay a player of Tracey's choice, to stand next to them when they were 'at it' and wave a towel close to her face. This would create a refreshing breeze to relax her, and she could look at his body and fantasize about it as Tudor was 'going about his 'business'.

Both Tudor and Tracey thought this was a marvellous idea, and they went to the rugby club to select their 'aide'.

Back at Tudor's mansion, the three got into position and made a start. The rugby player stood there, waving the towel, as agreed, and she ogled his muscular shape throughout the whole session. This happened about a dozen times, and Tudor was a bit disappointed to hear that Tracey was still not over ecstatic about their love-life.

The next time the rugby player arrived, Tracey suggested that they try something else – why don't they switch roles? Tudor could wave the towel and the rugby player could adopt Tudor's role in the lovemaking act.

All three agreed and they set about it. The rugby player seemed to be doing a good job, and Tudor frantically waved the towel throughout the whole episode. When it was all over, Tudor asked Tracey if that was any better. She said it was the most fantastic experience she'd ever had. Tudor was chuffed to beans with this, and, as the rugby player was leaving, Tudor shouted,

"See, lad, *that's* the way to wave a towel."

Another story tells of the farmer who tried to supplement his very low income by setting up a 'day out' service, whereby schools from towns and cities could visit the farm for a day, experience the rural environment and come into contact with animals. It was very popular and the farm was booked up for the whole of the school year.

One school party arrived, and the teacher who accompanied the children was a bit of a character. In his spare time, he was a children's entertainer, and he did card tricks, ventriloquism, impressions etc, at kiddies' parties.

The farmer led the party into the cowshed, the first port of call on the guided tour. As soon as the teacher entered, he used his ventriloquism skills to amuse the kids by having a conversation with a large Friesian. The teacher spoke first,

"Okay?"

"Yeah, not too bad, thanks."

"Busy?"

"No, not really. Travelled far, have you?"

"Well, we're from a North London Comp, so it's taken us about four hours to get here."

As the conversation developed, the farmer stood in amazement. The kids thought it was great, but the farmer was keen to move on, so he ushered them towards the pig sty. As soon as they arrived, the teacher engaged himself in conversation with one of the pigs.

"Lovely day?"

"Doesn't make much difference to us in here, mate!"

"Don't you get out much?"

"Never; stuck in here all the time."

"What do you do with yourselves all day?"

"Just hang about until grub time…"

Once again, the astonished farmer was eager to move on. He couldn't understand what was going on, and he seemed to be extremely 'on edge'. As they were walking across the farmyard, they noticed a sheep coming towards them. The farmer froze, and in a state of utter panic, turned round and screamed to the school party,

"Right! Let's get one thing straight before we go any further. If that sheep says *anything* about me, it's a bloody liar!"

I think there may be quite a lot of scope for gossip in *that* story!

* * *

Another story tells of a gentleman seeking medical advice on how to spruce up his love life. He told his doctor that it had been *years* since he had made love to his wife, and wondered if there was something that he could take to make things improve. The doctor informed the gentleman that the best thing he could take was lots of exercise, as he was grossly overweight and this was surely affecting his performance. He advised the gentleman to run ten miles a day for the next fortnight and to ring him in two weeks to report on his condition.

Two weeks later, the doctor's telephone rang. He picked it up.

"Hi, Doc, it's me. I've done what you said. I've run ten miles a day for the last fourteen days."

"Excellent news. Have you lost any weight?"

"Oh aye, I reckon about three stone, doctor."

"Are you making love to your wife again?"

"No."

"Why not?"

"Because I'm 140 miles away!"

* * *

Another tale tells of a Dad trying to protect his daughter's honour. You see, he lived next door to an American Air Base, and his three daughters were seeing USAF pilots. Early one evening, he was reading the *Western Mail*, when he heard a knock at the door. When he answered it, he was met by a big American guy, looking very smart in his uniform. Dai asked the American what he wanted. The Yank's reply was:

"Hi, sir, the name's Vance,

I've come to see Nance,

To take her to the dance.

What's the chance?"

Before Dai could say a word, Nance pushed her way passed him with a "Tara, Dad. See you after."

Dai returned to the *Western Mail*, and before he had time to open it, another knock came on the door. Once again, he met a very smart American, who said:

"Hi sir, the name's Joe.

I've come to see Flo,

To take her to the show.

I'm ready to go."

Before Dai could say a word, Flo pushed her way passed him with a,

"Tara, Dad. See you after."

This time, he didn't even get as far as the *Western Mail* before another knock came at the door. Strangely enough, he was greeted by a smartly dressed American, who announced

"Hi sir, the name's Buck…"

And before poor old Buck could utter another word, Dai screamed "She's out!" at him and slammed the door.

A bit hasty, I thought. Now we'll never know what plans Buck had for the evening.

* * *

Iolo, who lived in the same village, was besotted with Julie, who worked in the Grocer's. He had always fancied her but could never find the words to tell her how he felt. One thing he enjoyed doing was watching the shop, to see if any USAF pilots went in there, as he was very impressed with their patter. As soon as they went in the shop, he'd follow, hoping to pick up a couple of tips. On the day in question, one airman walked up to the counter, put his hand on Julie's and uttered in a deep sexy voice, "Hi, Honey, got any honey?"

Julie almost melted at this and shyly pointed out the shelf that contained the honey.

Iolo was very impressed with this, and he noticed the effect it had on Julie.

The next airman approached the counter, blew a kiss towards Julie and whispered, "Hi Sugar, got any sugar?"

Julie almost collapsed with emotion, and only just managed to point the airman in the direction of the sugar shelf before she had to go and have a sit down.

Iolo had noticed a pattern! He planned his move, and, when the airmen had left, he decided to put it into action.

He strode up to the counter, grabbed Julie by the hair and pulled her towards him. He planted a great big smacker on her lips and said, "Give us half a pound of bacon, you big fat pig."

* * *

Another strange tale tells of two lads waiting to meet their girlfriends outside the cinema. They've both been there for a while and they're getting restless.

"Late, is she?"

"Aye, always late."

"So's mine."

"Which film are you seeing?"

"Dunno, the horror, probably; she like the horror ones."

"Mine's the same. Funny, they usually like the weepies, don't they?"

"Well, my girlfriend works in the hospital; probably has enough of weeping all day. That's why she prefers the horror, see."

"Oh, mine works in the hospital, too."

"Hang on; she's just got off the bus."

"Aye, and mine, too."

As the young lady approaches, she suddenly realises that she's arranged to meet *both* her boyfriends outside the cinema. What's more, they're talking to each other! She decides it's best to face the music. The lads continue talking as she approaches.

"Where's your's then?"

"By there, look."

"What? Her with the red coat on?"

"Aye."

"The one coming towards us?"

"Aye."

"Well that's my girlfriend, too!"

"Hey, we're related!"

"What do you mean *related*?"

"Boyfriends-in-law, mun!"

Well, what a coincidence! And talking about coincidences, how about this tail-end of a conversation overheard in a local supermarket:

"… aye, her old man was on the buses for years."

"Big bloke, wasn't he?"

"No, tiny, he was. You're thinking of Bob, her second husband. He was a lorry driver."

"Wasn't he the one who played darts for the club?"

"Who now?"

"Her second husband."

"No, never played darts. Pool he always played. Played for the team, I think."

"For the club?"

"No, the Social. Always in the Social, he was. Never went in the club."

"Dark, wasn't he."

"No, very fair. Well, before he lost it, that is.

"I know him. Kept birds, didn't he?"

"No, never had birds."

"Didn't they have a caravan at Porthcawl?"

"No, it was her sister's. They used to go there on holiday, but it wasn't theirs."

"My sister had a caravan down Porthcawl."

"Never. Small world, innit?"

"Aye. You wouldn't believe it, would you?"

"Aye, that's a fact, it is."

* * *

On the whole, to avoid being the topic of any gossip, it's best to remain 'squeaky clean'. Don't get involved in any activities that may be adjudged abnormal, and if you do, make sure you don't get spotted. The one thing that you will have to look forward to will be the 'switch' to someone else, when news gets around that that 'someone else' has been involved in something even more heinous than your misdemeanour, and the interest and gossip moves over to them.

It may be a couple of days before something else 'raises its head', or it may take months. If you are getting a little bit impatient that nothing is going on that is likely to take the pressure off you, it may be worth considering 'cooking up something'. This could involve partaking in fact-finding missions, to root out any 'goings on' that are worth throwing onto the grapevine, or, more commonly, fabricating something from scratch, in order to create a diversion that occupies the interest of the gossips and will, in turn, mean that they will focus all their efforts into 'finding out more', taking you out of the spotlight.

"I see that that massage parlour in Newport is offering a little more than just massages, then."

"Where's that, then?"

"Dunno, thought you may have known. Apparently, half the blokes in the village use it regularly."

"Who are they, then?"

"Dunno, ask Tom, he knows, he's a regular – he told me."

"Tom who?"

"Tom… er… I think I've said enough already. I don't want to get anyone into trouble, like."

Managers

Managers are another group of characters who are well worth a look at. Since the demise of the pits in the valleys, companies have sprung up all over the place, in purpose-built industrial estates, and many of the people who worked in mining are now employed by these companies, producing all sorts of things.

It would take too long to go through a list of all the things that are manufactured and the services that are available from these industrial estates, but a quick flick through a local telephone directory will give you some idea of the hundreds of establishments that exist. One thing that they all have in common – they will all have a manager.

Most villages will also have a manager living within its boundaries – usually in the big 'new' houses that have sprung up above the existing terraces that used to house the miners and their families. Although their places of residence are generally more salubrious than the others in the village, the managers will mix with the villagers. For some reason, however, they tend to stand out.

Let's see if we can find out why.

Firstly, look at the car that the manager will be driving. It will be considerably more 'flash' than the vehicles owned by the rest of the villagers. It will be registered under the latest 'letter' for the year, and this will be changed when the next letter becomes the current one. No one in the village will be able to 'keep up with this', of course; and that's because they have to buy and maintain their own vehicles. As a result, villagers will also take better care of their vehicles than those who have theirs provided for them.

Flash cars being driven through villages at high speed, screeching to a halt outside the chip shop, on double yellow lines, will almost certainly be driven by managers. After a brief stop at the chippy, the car will 'take off', usually with a wheel spin, and screech to a halt ten yards further on, whilst the driver pops into the newsagents. This procedure usually lasts for about half a dozen stops, and represents a total distance of about 25 yards travelled. When the procedure is over, the vehicle will head off, at twice the speed limit, in the direction of the driver's house.

It is unlikely that there will be anyone in the village that wouldn't have noticed the vehicle and commented:

- "Blinkin' ridiculous, driving round the place like that!"

- "Parked on double yellow lines five times, then!"
- "And on a bend, too!"
- "Why couldn't he have just walked to the other shops, instead of having to drive to each one?

And more importantly:

- "Nice car, that, innit?"
- "Brand new, it is"
- "Must've cost a fortune!"
- "Still, he's got plenty of money, hasn't he? He can afford it." (Probably the most important.)

Managers are even easier to spot from their language and the things they talk about.

The language is very strange. Someone who does not come into contact with them may find it very difficult to ascertain exactly what the manager is talking about.

A typical manager may come out with something like "Hey, sorry, I've been chasing you for a while, but I needed to tie in with you so we could touch base. Now that we're all on board, I can get my guys moving and make sure we're all singing from the same song sheet, so to speak."

Conversations will be dominated by their work; what they do, and how difficult it is; the situations that arise during the course of a day, and how expertly they dealt with them, and bonuses, targets, perks, pressure, holidays, and, most importantly, how much their salary is.

Common terms to look out for:

- "I shouldn't be here now. I was supposed to be having an early night. I've got a meeting in London at 9am tomorrow. Oh, go on, then. I'll have another one."
- "So, I sacked the lot of 'em. Well, I didn't like doing it, but the directive came from above."

- "Well, the cock-up actually cost the company £15,000. I accepted full responsibility for it, although it wasn't my fault, and the loss was written off. I'll sort out those responsible in the morning. Heads will roll!"

- "We had a great meal. It's a bit expensive there but I love good food. The bill only came to £670 for four of us, but we did have two bottles of wine, so it wasn't bad, really."

- "Yes, we're going to cruise the Caribbean this year; thought we'd have a change, since we did the Maldives last year."

- "I'm going to the FA Cup final next week. Don't want to go. Corporate hospitality do, see. Important customers coming down. I'll hate it."

- "Well, I shouldn't really. Did I mention I had to be in London at 9am tomorrow? Oh, go on then, I'll have a quickie."

- "Don't worry, I'll order you one on the company credit card tomorrow. Pay me back when you can."

- "Okay, then, I may as well have one for the road. I've got to be in London by…"

- "Yeah, just jot your CV down on a piece of paper and I'll get my secretary to type it out for you tomorrow."

- "Pop your microwave down in the morning, leave it in reception, and I'll tell the electricians to have a look at it for you. Oh, thanks, go on, then; last one – I have to be in London by 9am tomorrow."

Directors

Directors are very similar to managers, but display an all round higher profile. To understand how the director works, read the managers' section again and substitute the key words as shown in the table below:

Manager	*Director*
Flash car (Rover, MR2)	Flasher Car (Merc, BMW)
Big new houses	Bigger newer houses
Twice the speed limit	Four times the speed limit
Meal only cost £670	Meal only cost £1200
Going to FA Cup final	Going to the Superbowl then on to Hong Kong Sevens
Caribbean cruise	Round the world, twice
London by 9am	Geneva/Paris/New York by 9am
	(*Delete as applicable*)

Them what went away and came back

This is a very strange phenomenon. It concerns people who have been born and nurtured in the valleys and have 'moved away', only to return a few years later. The most common cases are those who go to University. They attend their local school and move on to the local college, until they have amassed enough GCSE's and A-levels to enable them to go away to the University of their choice. On average, they spend three years, possibly more, 'away', and come back home. The odd thing is that the accent that took eighteen years to cultivate in their valley community will have completely disappeared in only three years of being away from it. Ah, I hear you say, if someone goes to Manchester for three years, they're bound to pick up a bit of a Coronation Street 'twang', or someone who went to London may use a bit of Cockney. It's only natural isn't it?

That may be. The strange thing is, though, regardless of where they went, be it London, Newcastle, Manchester, Leeds,

Glasgow, Belfast, Bristol, or even Cardiff, the accent they come back with will be the same one! It will be the accent used by TV newsreaders and presenters, with not a hint of any regional twangs or drawls, and commonly known as 'Posh'. It has always been a mystery to me why this happens, and it may well warrant further investigation – but not here.

I have noticed, though, that people who come home 'talking posh', are more inclined to frequent the restaurants frequented by managers, than stand in the street eating pasties and chips out of yesterday's *Argus,* with the mates that they had before they 'went away'.

Charity Shop Characters

Charity shops are marvellous places; marvellous for both characters and stuff. The stuff available in charity shops has to be seen to be believed. You can buy anything you need, if you visit half a dozen or so and are prepared to plough through each shop's entire stock. You'll find no-end of stuff that you can't believe that you've managed to survive as long as you have without owning, and, when you get home, you won't be able to believe what you've bought. Your newly acquired items will go straight into the 'for the charity shop box', to be taken back there as soon as it is full!

I bought a 'book-rest for an exercise-bike', during one of my charity shop reconnoitres. The fact that I don't own an exercise-bike made no difference to the fact that 'I just had to have it'. It wasn't until I got it home that I realised that I had no use for it at all, as my partner so vehemently pointed out. It is now *cwtshed* in a drawer. I managed to sneak it in there, in preference to the 'for the charity shop box', on the basis that I'll find a use for it one day, even if it means buying an exercise-bike, purely for the purpose of being able to read something as I'm peddling away, thanks to my superb bargain at the charity shop.

It is interesting to look at the way in which charity shop personnel price their goods. There seems to very little relationship between the actual value of their items and the prices that they are given. You can pay anything up to £5.99 for a *Greatest Love Songs* CD that was given away free in one of last week's Sunday papers, and for about 50p you can buy a very rare and sought-after 1970s progressive rock vinyl LP that will fetch at least £400 on E bay.

I have spent hours sifting through boxes of LPs in charity shops, and it's quite amazing what you can find. Quite amazing, in fact, to look at the number of albums that have been available, and they crop up all the time in charity shop LP sections. Take for example *Hammond Organ Classics*, where you can sit back and relax to the strains of the likes of Tchaikovsky, Beethoven, Bach and Vivaldi, all played on the Hammond organ. Or, there is *Hawaiian Guitar Classics*, where you can sit back and relax to the strains of… yes, honest! There are *Grecian Evenings*, where you can sit back and listen to all of the classic renditions, as played on the Hammond organ, or Hawaiian guitar, only this time, on the bouzouki.

One of my favourites is *The Best of Torville and Dean*. This is a double album and is normally the highest priced in the 'LP box'. I have always thought that the attraction of Torville and Dean was a purely visual thing, and I can't quite see how this can be captured enough to do it justice on a record. I can't imagine someone listening to this album, particularly *Bolero*, and thinking, "Cor, how's that for a triple Salchow!"

Perhaps the most amazing thing about these albums is

the very fact that they are in charity shops; which means that someone, somewhere, has actually gone out and bought them in the first place!

Characters that frequent charity shops are very varied. There are those who genuinely support whichever charity the shop represents, and buy as much as they can from the charity shops, even though they can often buy similar items more cheaply from ordinary high street outlets. Many charity shops produce greetings cards that bear their logos, and these are very popular with people who are of a naturally charitable nature.

There are those who rifle through the clothes and buy the most outrageous dresses, shoes and hats to use as outfits for fancy dress parties, and usually return them on the Monday, rather more 'stained' than they were before they purchased them.

There are those who rifle through the clothes and buy the most outrageous dresses, shoes and hats to use as outfits, under the guise of being for fancy dress parties, and never return them because they wear them when they go out – and are often heard bragging in pubs, "You'll never guess; I got the complete outfit from the charity shop! Only cost me £1.50 for the lot!"

A quick glance around at their listeners' faces will confirm that they *had* guessed that the outfit came from the charity shop, and that the £1.50 charged was nothing less than extortionate!

Then, there are the 'Wheelers and Dealers', who scour the shops for china and jewellery, in the hope that they will find a 'rare piece' that will sell for a massive profit on E bay. They usually know nothing about the pieces that they buy, and end up buying lots of stuff, most of which is worthless. They are usually loathe to 'give' these items back to charity shops, and try to sell them at car boot sales, generally for a loss. The one piece that will be 'worth a bit', out of the boxfuls of rubbish they try to shift at boot sales, is normally snapped up for 50p very quickly by 'those that know', and it will be sold on *Bargain Hunt* or at Sotheby's for hundreds of thousands of pounds.

One such wheeler and dealer contacted Sotheby's to report that he'd bought a Rembrandt and a Stradivarius from his local charity shop. They were very excited to hear this and sent an expert down to view the potentially very valuable items. They went back to London after informing the distraught wheeler and dealer that "Rembrandt made awful violins and Stradivarius was a crap painter."

Never mind.

The staff in charity shops always seem to have one predicament, whichever shop you go into. The till causes more problems than any other item that you find in a charity shop. It can be quite annoying. When you have selected two LP's, costing 50p each, you give the lady behind the counter £1, and then wait twenty minutes for your receipt and bag. As soon as the 'server' touches the till, it will bleep, flash, and start whirring and clanking uncontrollably. Just as you think things are settling down, the till roll will belch out yards of paper, usually blank, and the money drawer will fail to open.

After several attempts to open till, which consists of frantic pressing of buttons and the release of several more yards of blank receipts, the shop assistant will give up and shout to someone 'upstairs' to come down and sort it out.

Shortly, another person will appear, and this is usually the only person on the premises who knows how to operate the till. This person will gather up the till roll and wind it back onto its spindle, press one button, and the transaction will be completed in about four seconds. During the process, the 'expert' will huff and puff and smile politely at irate customers, with a look that suggests that this event has occurred at least ten times – in the last hour!

The expert will then march back upstairs, whilst the poor, apologetic assistant tries to work out how much change you should get for your pound, when you've just bought two albums for 50p each, before tearing off your foot-long receipt, even though the details of your purchase take up less than two inches.

Black Dogs

A Black Dogs, or Black Cats, depending on where you live, is a term used for someone who will outdo anyone who claims that they own, or have done, something special. The name derives from the comment, "If you've got a black dog/cat, he'll have a blacker one!"

You won't beat Black Dogs, no matter how hard you try, or how obscure your claims, which he will *have* to beat. So, if you claim to have a guitar that's seven feet long, four feet wide, with nine necks, the black dog will have a case to fit it.

If you've bought an Aston Martin DB6 for £15, the Black Dog would have bought one, full of tenners, for a fiver. He won't even beat you on bargains; no, sir, he'll beat you on anything.

"Spent £850 for your new PC, eh? Huh, mine cost £2000; mind you, it's smack up to date; not like that thing you've got!"

Don't even try calling the Black Dog's bluff, because it won't work. You will never see any evidence to support Black Dogs' claims.

Should you offer to buy his case for your extremely odd, nine-necked guitar (which, by the way, you made up), he'll promise to drop it round your house, for you to have a look at it. When he doesn't arrive, you'll ring him to find out where he is, only to be given the disastrous news that, unbeknown to him, his missus flogged it to a tinker only yesterday. But, never fear, he's pretty certain there's another one in the shed and he'll dig it out – oh, hang on a minute, his son has just informed him that the shed is on fire!

Strangely enough, it is not only humans that suffer Black Dogs!

There was a chicken and a frog, who were big mates. They went everywhere together. Although they were never apart, the chicken, secretly, hated the frog – because he was a Black Dog! Whatever the chicken had done, the frog had done it better. If the chicken had been to America, the frog had been there twice. The chicken couldn't stand it any longer.

One day, the chicken found out that the frog couldn't read. He enrolled for a reading course in the local college and didn't tell the frog what he had done. Six months later, the chicken could read and couldn't wait to tell the frog about it.

It was a Friday night; the chicken went to the pub, with a book under his wing. He looked in through the window and saw that the frog was already in there, sitting at a table, supping his pint. The chicken strode proudly up to the bar and ordered his drink. He walked into the lounge, put his drink next to the frog's, and sat down. Proudly, he took the book from under his wing, and put in on the table, right under the frog's nose. The frog looked at the book, then at the chicken. The chicken pointed at the book and said, "Book, book, book, book."

To which the frog replied, "Read it, read it, read it, read it."

On the whole, the best plan is to avoid Black Dogs. You'll never beat them. Don't even bother yourself by trying.

People at Bus Stops

People at bus stops can cause massive irritation to those who do not know how to deal with them properly.

Sometimes, if you are walking somewhere that is a fair distance away, and the weather suddenly looks as if it's going to take a turn for the worse, you may consider taking the bus instead. You don't know what time the buses go, but you espy a bus stop nearby, occupied by one person, who is obviously waiting for a bus. You approach the bus stop and look to see if there is a timetable pasted up somewhere. There is, but it has been severely scrawled on in thick black marker, so you can't read it. So, you ask the person who was at the bus stop when you arrived, if there is a bus due – a fatal mistake.

A typical reply to this will be, "Should be anytime now. I've been here for ten minutes, so it shouldn't have gone."

This is good enough, a straight question and a straight answer. The trouble is, once you've made the initial contact, people at bus stops then feel compelled to engage you in conversation until the bus arrives!

Usual follow ups are:

- "The trouble is: I think they run to suit themselves these days."
- "You wait for an hour, then six turn up at the same time. Ought to stagger them, they did."
- "I don't know why they have a timetable there; they don't stick to it, anyway. Not that you can read it – blinkin' kids.

Scribbled all over it, they have. I blame the parents."

When all bus times and the state of the bus stop have been covered, up crops the all-time favourite – the weather.

- "Looks like we're going to have a drop of rain."
- "Let's hope it holds off till the bus comes."
- "Didn't expect rain today. It was quite bright his morning, and they never said nothing about rain on the forecast this morning."
- "I should have worn my coat. Would have, if I'd known."
- "You wouldn't believe it was June, would you? It's like winter! Bloomin' ridiculous, it is. That's deodorant that causes that, you know. Blinking scientists! Never had that with the roll-on. Can't get them anymore. It's all in cans now, see."

And so it continues until the bus arrives.

Safe? Not yet, time for one more. Not only are buses the biggest vehicles on the road and highly recognisable, but people at bus stops will offer the final piece of information, just before you get on. As it pulls into the stop, just in case you have not caught on, they will say, "Ah, here it is. It hadn't gone."

Whilst you have been a saint, by nodding and smiling politely throughout the onslaught that you've put up with at the bus stop, there is a further potential danger. If you get on the bus first, your new friend may decide to sit by you and continue the conversation for the duration of the journey. To combat this, make sure that you let them get on the bus first, and when they are sitting down, go and sit somewhere else.

This works most of the time, but in extreme cases, some

have noticed that you are sitting somewhere else and have left their seat to come to sit by you. This is worse, because now you are blocked in!

Don't worry; this scenario can be avoided by following these quick and easy steps.

(1) Ask the person at the bus stop if a bus is due.
(2) Wait for the reply.
(3) Wait a bit longer, to see if there is going to be any follow-up.
(4) If there is no follow-up (doubtful), wait for the bus.
(5) If there is follow up, say, "I think I'll chance the rain, I fancy a walk."
(6) Walk slowly away from the bus stop, glancing back all the time, in case the bus comes.
(7) Stop when you are out of sight of the person at the bus stop, but near enough to be able to get back to it when the bus arrives.
(8) When the bus arrives, wait until the person gets on, and then run towards the bus, with your left arm sticking out.
(9) When paying the driver, glance around the bus, locate the offending person, and plan where you are going to sit.
(10) Scrap all of the above and walk anyway.

Conclusion

We have looked at valley characters in some detail. We have not explored individual characters. Every village will have a main 'character', who will be known to all and will have certain traits peculiar to him/her.

To investigate these individuals would be an impossible task, as we would have to address every village in turn and look at each character. In which case, this book would be longer than *War and Peace* and still wouldn't do each character justice. Instead, we have looked at groups of characters, and tried to understand the way they operate to allow us all to live together in peace and harmony. Of course, pedigree valley people will be fully aware of these traits and will carry on their lives as normal.

The difficulty is that valley towns are becoming more popular with visitors from 'elsewhere'. Most villages are within a stone's throw of major areas of outsta-nding natural beauty, or tourist attractions, and it is important that visitors have a broad knowledge of the locals, in order to survive their stays.

I have quite often heard visitors say, "Oh, the locals are so friendly here! So different from the folk in London. I don't even know my next door neighbour there, but they're so nice down here. It's marvellous!"

So, a visitor who is camping on the mountainside and has visited a local shop will have been subjected to:

"So, where are you from, then?"

"What are you doing here?"

"How long are you here for?"

"Married?"

"What do you do for a living, then?"

The visitors love it. So do the locals. The best bit is when one of the visitors ventures into the local for a pint and is spotted by one of the customers that grilled him in the shop earlier: "See him by there, he's a solicitor. On holiday, he is. From Leicester. Down here for a fortnight with his wife and kids. She's a nurse. Oi, Nigel, why don't you come over here and have a pint with us."

One rather disturbing illustration tells of a visiting couple who popped into the local pub. After the initial introductions, one man invited them to his home, saying, "I'm a Cordon Bleu chef, my wife is a Cordon Bleu chef, my daughter is a pastry chef and my son is a connoisseur of fine wine. Why don't you pop around for an evening of fine wine and top class food?

The visitors were overwhelmed with the generosity and accepted gracefully.

Another man standing at the bar said, "I'm a concert pianist, my wife plays the cello, my son plays the viola and my daughter plays the violin. Why not pop around one evening for some excellent music and chat?"

Once again, they accepted.

Another man, on hearing this and not wishing to be outdone piped up, "I'm an all-in wrestler, my wife is the Welsh female boxing champion, my son is a master of Kung Fu and my daughter has a black belt in Karate. Why not pop round our house one evening, and we'll kick your teeth in?"

I'm not sure if they accepted the last offer.

So, to recap, let's look at the facts of the matter and ask these questions :

- Do you spend more than four nights a week in the pub?
- Do you favour the club?
- Do you favour the pub?
- Have you been up in front of the committee?
- Have you been banned/had your beer stopped?
- Have you sat in someone else's seat?
- Have you bought something in a pub?
- Did you find out, later, that the thing you bought was stolen?
- Did you keep shtoom, even though you knew the owner?
- Have you been given advice by a pub expert?
- Did you heed that advice?
- Are you a pub expert?
- Did you know anything about the subject that you gave advice on?
- Did the person you gave advice to heed it?
- Is that person still speaking to you?
- Have you ever asked a builder to do a job for you?
- Did he turn up?
- Did you have to go out and buy more tea and biscuits after the builder left your house?
- Did you ever pay a builder before he'd finished the job?
- Are you still speaking to him?
- Do you have a computer?
- Have you ever asked a computer expert for help?
- Are you still speaking to him?
- Have you ever given a more ridiculous answer in a pub quiz than any of those shown in the quiz section?
- Have you ever been gossiped about?

- Have you ever gossiped about someone else?
- Have you ever started a rumour to get yourself off the hook?
- Have you ever started a rumour purely to wind up known gossips?
- Does a manager/director live near you?
- Is his car better than yours?
- Ever been out for a meal with a manager/director?
- Did he pay?
- Are you still speaking to him?
- Did you go to University or move away for some other reason?
- When you came back, did you sound like someone in *Midsomer Murders*?
- Why? (Answer this in full if you answered 'yes' to the previous question)
- Do you frequent charity shops?
- Do you buy from charity shops in order to make money?
- Do you buy the clothes that you wear every day from charity shops?
- Have you been kept for longer than an hour in a charity shop, waiting for your change?
- Do you know someone who has a black dog?
- Is yours blacker?
- Do you feel compelled to beat anything people say to you?
- Have you ever been accosted on a bus stop?
- Did you handle it well? (If you answered 'yes' to the previous question)
- Have you been accosted and still travel on buses?

If you answered 'yes' to more than twenty of these, you are a true valley person.

If you answered 'yes' to between ten and fifteen of these you should get by in the valleys.

If you answered 'yes' to less than ten of these, you are a visitor and have never been to the valleys.

If you answered 'no' to more than 40% of these then you may seriously consider whether you should be thinking of coming to the valleys.

Don't be silly, come on up; you'll get a *cwtsh* from us, all the same.

Welsh Valleys Humour

David
Jandrell

A first-time visitor to the south Wales Valleys will be subjected to a language that will initially be unfamiliar to them. This book features a tongue-in-cheek guide to the curious ways in which Valleys inhabitants use English, together with anecdotes, jokes, stories depicting Valleys life, and malapropisms from real-life Valleys situations!

"What a delight David Jandrell's book is!"
– **Ronnie Barker**

£3.95
ISBN: 0 86243 736 9

The *It's Wales* series is just one of
a whole range of Welsh interest
publications from Y Lolfa. For a full list
of books currently in print, send now for
your free copy of our new, full-colour
Catalogue – or simply surf into our
website, **www.ylolfa.com**, for secure,
on-line ordering.

y|**L**o*lfa*

Talybont, Ceredigion, Cymru SY24 5AP
e-bost ylolfa@ylolfa.com
gwefan www.ylolfa.com
ffôn (01970) 832 304
ffacs 832 782